YOUNG ADULT
HEARING GOD'S VOICE

STUDY GUIDE

ZOE Ministries International

ACKNOWLEDGMENTS

ZOE Ministries International is dedicated to training, equipping and sending believers into the world to minister by the leading of the Holy Spirit. This ministry helps build the body of Christ and encourages God's people to use their gifts and talents for His glory. It is for this purpose that this publication has been compiled by the leading of the Holy Spirit and the input of many people. ZOE Ministries wishes to thank them for their support, time, and talents in contributing to this Study Guide. We give our Lord all the praise and glory for this work!

CONTENTS

YOUNG ADULT HEARING GOD'S VOICE
COURSE OUTLINE

Lesson 1   **INTRODUCTION**

Main Principle: God wants all of His children to be disciples of Jesus and to hear, know and follow His voice. We can hear God's specific word for us in every area of our lives.

Article: "Salvation Scriptures" ZOE Ministries

Lesson 2   **INTRODUCTION (continued)**

Main Principle: God greatly desires to communicate and have fellowship with us. He speaks to us in our spirit. We may hear God through an inner knowing, the inner voice and the authoritative voice of the Holy Spirit.

Article: *Hearing The Voice Of God*, John Dawson

Lesson 3   **UNDERSTANDING GOD'S VOICE**

Main Principle: We must listen for God's voice in our spirit, and not be led astray by what others say nor depend totally on our own limited reasoning. As we hear and obey God's voice, we can participate in God's plans for the world. Following God's instructions will result in a positive impact on us and on our families.

Scripture: Genesis 6:5 through 8:22

Lesson 4   **SPIRIT, SOUL, BODY—WHAT'S THE DIFFERENCE?**

Main Principle: Since we hear God's voice in our spirits, we need to understand the differences between the spirit, soul and body.

Study Help: "Spirit, Soul, Body—What's the Difference?" ZOE Ministries

Lesson 5 **SPIRIT, SOUL, BODY—WHAT'S THE DIFFERENCE? Part 2**

Main Principle: We have the choice of listening to our spirit, which is directed by the Holy Spirit, or to our soul. Sometimes the soul can make it hard to hear and obey what God is saying in our spirit.

Article: *Hearing From God*, Billye Brim

Lesson 6 **OBEYING THE SPIRIT**

Main Principle: As we learn to obey the Holy Spirit, we will become more aware of how the Holy Spirit can minister through us.

Scripture: 2 Chronicles 19:1–11; 2 Chronicles 20:1–30

Article: *Twelve Points To Remember,* Points 1 and 2, Loren Cunningham
Study Help: "Obeying the Spirit," ZOE Ministries

Lesson 7 **WHAT KEEPS US FROM HEARING GOD'S VOICE?**

Main Principle: As we seek to hear God's voice more clearly, we will need to keep our hearts yielded toward the Lord. Sin in our life acts as a barrier to communication with God.

Scripture: 1 Samuel 10:1–10; 1 Samuel 13:1–14; 1 Samuel 15:1–35; 1 Samuel 16:1–13

Study Help: "What Keeps Us From Hearing?" ZOE Ministries
Article: *Forgiving My Father*, Josh McDowell

Lesson 8 **DIFFERENT WAYS GOD SPEAKS—INNER KNOWING**

Main Principle: The inner knowing is a common way God leads us. It can take the form of a "knowing that you know," a holy hunch, a sudden uneasiness, a sense of peace or a caution.

Scripture: Acts 16:1–15; Acts 20:13–38; Acts 21:1–16

Study Help: "Inner Knowing," ZOE Ministries
Articles: *Twelve Points To Remember*, Points 3, 4 and 5 (Refer to Lesson 6 pages 47-48)
             Death Camp Revisited, Corrie ten Boom

Lesson 9   DIFFERENT WAYS GOD SPEAKS—INNER VOICE

Main Principle: God can communicate with us through the inner voice, which is quiet guidance with words. This still, small voice is the gentle whisper of the Holy Spirit in our spirit.

Scripture: Acts 4:32 through Acts 5:16

Articles: *When God Says, "Wait"*, Iverna Tompkins
            Twelve Points To Remember Points 6, 7 and 8 (Refer to Lesson 6 pages 47-48)

Lesson 10   DIFFERENT WAYS GOD SPEAKS—AUTHORITATIVE VOICE OF THE HOLY SPIRIT

Main Principle: The Holy Spirit can speak with words that seem to be audible to people nearby. What He says will never contradict Scripture.

Scripture: 1 Samuel 3

Article: *Twelve Points To Remember*, Points 9 and 10 (Refer to Lesson 6 pages 47-48)

Lesson 11   OTHER MANIFESTATIONS OF THE HOLY SPIRIT

Main Principle: God can communicate with us through dreams, visions and other manifestations of the Holy Spirit.

Scripture: Acts 9:1–19; Acts 10:1–48

Article: *Twelve Points To Remember*, Points 11 and 12 (Refer to Lesson 6 pages 47-48)
Study Help: "Review of Hearing God's Voice" ZOE Ministries
Article: *Hearing God's Voice*, Don Williams

Lesson 12   GO TELL!

Main Principle: As we remember what Jesus has done for us, we renew our determination to love and follow Him. As we recognize the gift of God within us, we are prepared to go out into the world and bring the good news of reconciliation with God the Father through Jesus by the power of the Holy Spirit.

Scripture: John 20:1–23

Articles: *The New Breed of World Changers*, Nevers Mumba
            "ZOE Course Descriptions" ZOE Ministries

Dear Participant,

We are so pleased that you will be going through ZOE's Young Adult Hearing God's Voice course. This is an exciting course that has been adapted from the adult curriculum for you.

As we examine the Scripture John 10:27, "My sheep hear my voice, and I know them, and they follow me (KJV)," we realize that when Jesus was saying this, He may not have been directing it only to His disciples. There were probably young adults within earshot of His voice. We believe the Lord wants to and does speak to His children of all ages.

Jesus made an incredible statement in John 14:11-12: "Believe me when I say that I am in the Father and the Father is in me; or at least believe on the evidence of the miracles themselves. *I tell you the truth, anyone who has faith in me will do what I have been doing. He will do even greater things than these, because I am going to the Father.*" [our emphasis added]

As you stay open to the work of the Lord, this course will equip you to partner with Jesus in establishing His kingdom on earth.

It is our prayer that the Holy Spirit will unlock your heart to better understand and recognize the voice of God. May God bless you and your friends as He unfolds His desire to be in deeper relationship with each of you.

In His Service,
Dick and Ginny Chanda
Founding Directors

A NOTE TO COURSE PARTICIPANTS

What ZOE Is!

1. A ministry that provides training for disciple-making.
2. Participatory courses where all are encouraged to share and contribute.
3. A situation where the leader (facilitator) decreases and the participants increase.
4. A drawing out of ministry gifts and preparation for the Lord's calling on individual lives.
5. A time when one can grow in the understanding and appreciation of others' gifts.
6. A safe environment in which an individual can feel comfortable to practice operating in his or her gifts.
7. A time of understanding the heart of the Father and applying that to one's life.

What ZOE Is Not!

1. A traditional Bible study.
2. A course where the leader speaks and the people take notes.
3. A place where people can air their opinions or gripes.
4. A place where people can discuss church doctrines.
5. A time when "weird" ministry happens.

A Reminder to Participants:

"A ZOE course is not just a Bible study; our leader is a facilitator and coach, not a teacher"

It is our desire that the Lord Jesus Christ be glorified in all that is said and done in ZOE courses. We wish to foster an understanding of the operation of His Holy Spirit and to yield to His workings.

PARTICIPANT'S RESPONSIBILITIES

I. Course Preparation

    A. Feel free to read the scriptures at home. As the scriptures are read aloud in class:

        1. Ask the Holy Spirit, **"Open my eyes that I may see wonderful things in Your law." Psalm 119:18.** You may be very familiar with the Scriptures, but the Lord is very faithful and can give you "fresh manna."

        2. Look at the Main Principle for the lesson and apply the Scriptures. Ask yourself the following questions:
            a. How does this Scripture apply to the lesson?
            b. How does this Scripture apply to my life?
            c. What do I need to do to apply this Scripture to my life and to the lives of others for God's glory?

    B. Maintain a journal—a valuable tool in God's hands.
As you learn to hear God's voice and keep a record of His speaking, you will become more aware of what He is saying to you and how He wants to work through you. See the article "Journaling—A Good Way to Hear God's Voice."

    C. Spend time in prayer.

        1. Prayer is valuable preparation for these courses. The more time you spend with the Lord, the more you will come to know Him.

        2. Spend time with God <u>daily</u>! God shows no partiality—what He has done for others, He will do for you! Growth will come as you respond to God's Holy Spirit at work in your life.

II. Course Participation

    A. Training is active! You will be encouraged to **take part in the course discussions and the prayer and ministry time.**

    B. Keep confidential everything that is shared during class.

JOURNALING – A GOOD WAY TO HEAR GOD'S VOICE

What Goes Into a Journal?

1. Your thoughts—impressions, insights, hopes, fears, goals, struggles
2. Your feelings—both positive and negative
3. Your prayers and answers to prayer
4. Excerpts from Scripture and other reading that God seems to be highlighting for you

How to Journal

1. You may choose to use a spiral binder or a hardback blank book, or anything that you can take with you easily on trips.
2. Journal every day, if possible, during the time that you read Scripture and pray. Record in it insights that the Lord gave you that day or the day before.
3. You may want to keep a separate section in your journal for prayers or excerpts from your reading.
4. Write directly to God as if you were talking to Him or writing Him a letter.

The Benefits of Keeping a Journal are Many

1. Journaling fosters a readiness to hear from God. Personal communion with God takes place as you write out your thoughts and feelings, and record the insights and impressions He gives you.
2. As you read God's Word and record your insights about Scripture, God is faithful to provide the admonitions, encouragement and guidance that you need.
3. Prayers become specific as you place them in print. In addition, God gets the glory when you review your journal and see your prayers have been answered.
4. Journaling helps clarify your thinking. Fears and struggles are more clearly defined so that they can be dealt with.
5. During times of discouragement, it can help to look back over your journal and see God's faithfulness and your progress in spiritual growth.

LESSON 1

INTRODUCTION

MAIN PRINCIPLE

God wants all of His children to be disciples of Jesus and to hear, know and follow His voice. We can hear God's specific word for us in every area of our lives.

YOUNG ADULT HEARING GOD'S VOICE
SALVATION SCRIPTURES

1.   Preparation for Salvation (being born again)

a. **John 3:16** "For God so loved the world that he gave his one and only Son, that whoever believes in him shall not perish but have eternal life."

b. **Romans 3:23** "...For all have sinned and fall short of the glory of God...."

c. **Romans 6:23** "For the wages of sin is death, but the gift of God is eternal life in Christ Jesus our Lord."

d. **John 1:12-13** "Yet to all who received him, to those who believed in his name, he gave the right to become children of God—children born not of natural descent, not of human decision or a husband's will, but born of God."

e. **John 7:37-39** "On the last and greatest day of the Feast, Jesus stood and said in a loud voice, 'If anyone is thirsty, let him come to me and drink. Whoever believes in me, as the Scripture has said, streams of living water will flow from within him.' By this he meant the Spirit, whom those who believed in him were later to receive. Up to that time the Spirit had not been given, since Jesus had not yet been glorified."

2.   Confession/Prayer

Romans 10:9-11 "That if you confess with your mouth, 'Jesus is Lord,' and believe in your heart that God raised him from the dead, you will be saved. For it is with your mouth that you believe and are justified, and it is with your mouth that you confess and are saved. As the Scripture says, 'Anyone who trusts in him will never be put to shame.'

3.   What Has Happened?

a. **Romans 10:13** "...For everyone who calls on the name of the Lord will be saved."

b. **Ezekiel 36:26-27** "I will give you a new heart and put a new spirit in you; I will remove from you your heart of stone and give you a heart of flesh. And I will put my Spirit in you and move you to follow my decrees and be careful to keep my laws."

4.   Follow-Up

a. Read the book of **John** or a pamphlet that would help you learn more about God and the new relationship you have with Him.

b. Talk with mature Christians to get answers to any questions and be encouraged by them. Go with them to church.

DISCLAIMER

The articles that follow have been chosen to give you, the reader, a broader perspective on many of the issues presented in the course. All the ideas in these articles do not necessarily represent the views of *ZOE Ministries International*. However, we pray that as you read and study, you will glean a sense of what is in the author's heart. At all times we need to ask the question, "Does this line up with the Word of God?"

LESSON 2

INTRODUCTION
(CONTINUED)

MAIN PRINCIPLE

God greatly desires to communicate and have fellowship with us. He speaks to us in our spirit. We may hear God through an inner knowing, the inner voice and the authoritative voice of the Holy Spirit.

HEARING THE VOICE OF GOD

by John Dawson

The people who have positively changed history have all had this in common: they obeyed the voice of God.

Divine guidance is partly a learned skill, an ongoing dialogue, a byproduct of devotion to and conversation with God.

God's goal is ultimately to conform us to the image of Jesus. Therefore, our daily decisions are to be firmly anchored in the biblical revelation of the character of God.

There are three great disciplines of any relationship: 1) presence—you have to be with the person; 2) shared responsibility; and 3) observation of character traits. And beyond these things, there are other conditions to consider when it comes to hearing the voice of God.

The first is a commitment to obedience. God will never give you additional direction so you can decide whether to obey Him. He wants to evaluate your commitment to obedience *before* He gives you further light, lest you come into greater judgment. Commitment means considering no other options. If you are committed to a task, you need to be doing it as though you were going to be doing it forever.

Secondly, we need to have a deep desire—not just a willingness through fear of the Lord—to yield to the Holy Spirit's direction. How

do you approach God's leadership? Do you approach God with your agenda? Or do you ask Him, "What do you think would be the very best for me?"

This world has yet to see what God can and will do through a totally yielded vessel. Yieldedness is a daily choice, a love response to God, not one climatic moment at an altar.

A lifetime of yieldedness only comes from having fallen in love with the qualities of God's holiness, His fairness, His justice and His gentleness. We abandon ourselves to Him again and again without risk, with the attitude of wanting to bring pleasure to His heart.

Part of yieldedness is being willing to wait and to trust His timing. Sometimes yieldedness demands going a step beyond the present resources; for faith only operates in the area beyond our information and ability.

The next condition of guidance is having a clear conscience before God and man. "If I regard iniquity in my heart, the Lord will not hear me" (Ps. 66:18).

And, finally, we need to practice daily the disciplines of the Holy Spirit. First of all is worship, just enjoying His presence (I Chron. 16:29). Second is waiting

on God, showing deference to the will and desire of the Lord (Ps. 37:7). Then, there are the meditation on His Word; the study of His character; the intercessory prayers; faith and self-control. All of these activities take place in the concept of the basic discipline of having an appointment with God every day. It is this daily seeking of God which reveals His maximum purpose for your life.

If you have a daily appointment with God, your priorities will be established. Your ministry must not come before fellowship with God. The Bible commands the wise man not to bask in his wisdom, nor the mighty man in his might, nor the rich man in his riches, but for them to boast in this alone, that they know God (Jer. 9:23,24).

One outstanding hero of walking and talking together with God is Enoch. One day as they were, perhaps, straining to communicate through the veil of the flesh, God said to him, "What was that? Come up here!" And they are still in conversation!

If you keep your appointments with God, it eliminates 95 percent of your temptations. The world does not have any allure for the one who has vital union with Jesus. Are you struggling with temptation? Then you are drifting from the daily loving presence of the Lord.

Also, if you have had an appointment with God, it removes any guilt about relaxation in the day. If you have grieved your most important relationship, you feel unfulfilled, a little awkward and are unable to enjoy fully any further pleasure.

Next, it eliminates boredom. The Bible states that to the rebellious, everything is boring. If you are in the straitjacket of pride, everything is boring; but there is a childlike joy, an exuberance of life which comes when we have communed with our heavenly Father.

Keeping your appointment with God gives your words penetrating power; it makes you sharp as a two-edged sword in counsel. People do not come to you just because you are wise. You are only as effective as you are yielded to Jesus and in touch with Him at the moment.

There are several ways in which you hear God speak directly. You may have a check, a conviction, a witness, or a leading of the Spirit: That is when the Spirit of God injects His wisdom into your stream of consciousness. Usually, the voice of God is not an external voice. When you yield your mind and spirit to Him consciously, He fills your thoughts with His wisdom which is always consistent with His Word and character.

Another manner in which the Holy Spirit speaks to you in your daily circumstances is through Bible reading and memorization. The Word of God in you is like a computer data base, on a hard disk, which the Spirit of God, the operating program, can work upon. If you have little scriptural data, then there is a limit to the wisdom God can minister to you.

Other ways of guidance are through the approval and blessing of spiritual leaders and through the gifts of the Spirit. But their ministry should be a confirmation of what God has already placed in your heart.

Another way God has spoken in the Word is by divine intervention. Balaam's donkey was strong guidance (Num. 22). Phillip's miraculous transportation was, no doubt, the most direct method of guidance (Acts 8:39). Such incidences are rarely seen; because the greatest hindrance to the miraculous is not lack of faith, but a lack of humility. No one wants to serve an apprenticeship. It seems everybody is self-realizing. We either call attention to the divine intervention and ourselves; or we do it on a more subtle level. What are the goals of the average believer? To overcome besetting sins; to have knowledge of the Word of God; to know his motivational gifts and temperament traits; to have complete inner healing; and to have wise and loving leadership to release him into his fullest potential. Jesus will lead you into those things, but our primary goal is to serve the Living God through steps of obedience.

///

DO YOU APPROACH GOD WITH YOUR AGENDA? OR DO YOU ASK HIM, "WHAT DO YOU THINK WOULD BE THE VERY BEST FOR ME?"

///

The next way of guidance is through visions and dreams. We see that Peter had a vision. Then we have angelic visitations; the first few chapters of Matthew are full of them. My wife experienced an angelic visitation in Ethiopia, as a missionary with Youth With A Mission. Out in the middle of a communist insurrection, that turned into a civil war, she became separated from her group. She was lonely and afraid; but an angelic messenger stood beside her bed and ministered peace to her.

Then we have an audible voice. Think of the baptism of Jesus; think of the story of Samuel—God spoke in an audible voice.

In regard to these things, we need to be aware of counterfeits. Don't seek a message; seek the Lord! Let me warn you about abusing the principle of putting out a fleece. A fleece can be an impersonal way of having God act on an inanimate object or through a circumstance; and it can deny a relationship with, or avoid an encounter with God. The fleece can be confirmation; but it should never be your sole direction or a way of life.

Lastly, we talk about the practical application of hearing God's voice. It is a spiritual skill; it is a discipline; it is a relationship; it is something we gain familiarity with, just as with another person's voice. You see there are really only three voices—man's, Satan's and God's.

To deal with your voice, you apply the truth of being crucified with Christ and say, "I delight to do your will, O God" (Ps. 40:8). You cannot, of course, crucify yourself. Dying to self is a step of faith; it is asking God to put to death the fears, imaginings, drives and appetites which would assert themselves. It is taking your hopes, aspirations, dreams, possessions, relationships and putting them on the altar as a living sacrifice. It is believing the Holy Spirit will keep them there. The voice you now hear, having checked its consistency with the Word, will be the direction of God. You see, it is a step of faith.

The same Living God, who flung the stars into space, who formed the majesty of the mountains, who calmed the incredible gale-force winds, has applied Himself to your life's direction! Therefore, it is safe to come to Him in total abandonment and trust...

—Excerpts from a message given at Christ For The Nations Institute

John Dawson is part of the leadership team for Youth With a Mission, an international missionary organization of Christians from many denominations dedicated to presenting Jesus Christ to this generation.

Reprinted by permission: Christ for the Nations

CFNI, P.O. Box 769000, Dallas, TX 75376-9000, 800-933-2364

LESSON 3

UNDERSTANDING GOD'S VOICE

MAIN PRINCIPLE

We must listen for God's voice in our spirit, and not be led astray by what others say nor depend totally on our own limited reasoning. As we hear and obey God's voice, we can participate in God's plans for the world. Following God's instructions will result in a positive impact on us and our families.

UNDERSTANDING GOD´S VOICE

Note: There are no articles for this Lesson

LESSON 4

SPIRIT, SOUL, BODY—WHAT'S THE DIFFERENCE?

MAIN PRINCIPLE

Since we hear God's voice in our spirits, we need to understand the differences between the spirit, soul and body.

YOUNG ADULT HEARING GOD'S VOICE

SPIRIT, SOUL, BODY—WHAT'S THE DIFFERENCE?

OUTLINE TO ACCOMPANY TEACHING

I. Definitions - 1 Thessalonians 5:23

A. Spirit -

B. Soul -

C. Body -

- - - - - - - - - -

D. Heart -

II. Differentiating between spirit and soul

A. Hebrews 4:12

B. 1 Corinthians 15:45-49

C. Matthew 10:39

III. Characteristics of spirit and soul

A. James 3:13-18

Soul -

Spirit -

B. Jude 17-21

Soul -

Spirit -

C. 1 Corinthians 2:7-16

Soul -

Spirit -

IV. How do we fine tune our spirit and eliminate the static of the soul?

    A. James 1:21

    B. Matthew 26:36-46

    C. Psalm 57:6-11

V. Areas of the soul to bring into submission

    A. Mind

    B. Will

    C. Emotions

VI. Summary

    A. Matthew 11:28-30

LESSON 5

SPIRIT, SOUL, BODY—WHO RULES?

MAIN PRINCIPLE

We have the choice of listening to our spirit, which is directed by the Holy Spirit, or to our soul. Sometimes the soul can make it hard to hear and obey what God is saying in our spirit.

HEARING FROM GOD

by Billye Brim

GOD WANTS YOU TO HEAR FROM HIM! HE HAS A PLAN FOR YOUR LIFE, AND HE WANTS YOU TO FULFILL THAT PLAN. HE SENT THE WONDERFUL HOLY GHOST TO INSTRUCT YOU IN HOW TO DO THAT. SO HE WANTS YOU TO HEAR FROM HIM EVEN MORE THAN YOU WANT TO HEAR!

In June 1989, I heard from God while I was at a camp meeting in Nashville, Tennessee. We were singing a song with the word "heart" in it. As I looked at that word on the overhead projector, the letters "e-a-r" popped out. And the Lord said to me, "The ear that you hear Me with is in the center of your heart. I put it there."

I had a knowing by the Spirit of the Lord that the ear of the Church is going to be opened for these last days. There is nothing more important for any of us in the church right now than to hear from God and obey Him.

All history hangs on two golden hooks: The first coming of the Lord and the Second Coming of the Lord. All other history pales in the light of those two events. And the Second Coming of the Lord is near. So God has a people, a Church, in the earth, whom He has cleansed with His blood and filled with His Spirit so we can hear Him and move in accordance with His divine will.

After that incident with the Lord, He took me to Proverbs 20:27. I knew it contained a key to hearing from him. "The spirit of man is the lamp of the LORD, searching all the inner depths of his heart." This lamp, your spirit, gives off light; it is the part of you that God uses to enlighten you, to guide you.

Man has a soul—the mind, will and emotions. He lives in a body, but he is a spirit. I Thessalonians 5:23 tells us we are spirit, soul and body.

The Bible also tells us it's not the house that contains good. That's why it doesn't do you any good to go to a palm reader. You're not going [to] touch God with your body. You can't depend on goose bumps for hearing from God. It's not your mind, your will or your emotions that touch God and hear from Him. It is your heart, the inward man of the heart—the Bible calls him the spirit man.

Inside of you, in the real you, is where God is going to speak and lead and guide. It is your spirit that He uses as a lamp to enlighten you so that you may know whom to marry, so that you know how to invest your money, so that you don't make bad mistakes.

People are carnal. They let their outer man dominate them. They spend all their time watching soap operas or Oprah or videos. You have to keep that inner man tuned to God if you want to hear Him in the smallest, most minor details of life.

God has a plan and a blueprint for each life He created. In the New Covenant, He's given us the indwelling Holy Spirit to interpret that plan for us. But we have to do it His way. We can't run to God for five minutes a day or one Sunday morning a week and one Wednesday night, be mean to our spouse, a grouch at the office, "veg out" in front of the television—and still hear from God! We have to do things God's way.

We are redeemed. "Christ hath redeemed us from the curse of the law, being made a curse for us: for it is written, Cursed is every one that hangeth on a tree, that the blessing of Abraham might come on the Gentiles through Jesus Christ; that we might receive the promise of the Spirit through faith" (Gal. 3:13,14 KJV).

Our redemption is threefold. You can only redeem something that you already owned. You can go to a pawn shop and redeem your wedding rings if you pawned them in a time of need. It means to buy back.

God made us. We were crowned with glory, but we fell from that glory when we walked into the hands of the enemy. However, God provided a Lamb to redeem us from the hand of the enemy. He translated us out of the kingdom. We're redeemed for a divine purpose.

ALL YOUR LIFE LONG, SATAN WILL BE TRYING TO DO ONE OF TWO THINGS — TO BRING THE CURSE ON YOU AND CHEAT YOU OUT OF YOUR BLESSINGS — YOUR INHERITANCE. BUT YOU CAN SAY TO HIM, BASED ON THE REDEMPTIVE BLOOD OF JESUS, "NO, YOU DON'T, SATAN. I'M REDEEMED BY THE BLOOD OF THE LAMB. YOU'RE NOT GOING TO KEEP ME AWAY FROM THE BLESSING OF GOD."

Galatians 3:13 tells us that Jesus Christ redeemed us from the curse of the law, from the hand of the enemy. And He's redeemed us to the blessing! There's an inheritance for the saints of God!

In the new covenant any man, woman, boy or girl can be born of the Spirit of God. Once we've been washed with the blood, the Holy Spirit dwells in us.

To hear from God, you need to cooperate with God's redemption plan. His blood washed you so that His Spirit can fill you. He can lead you and guide you and use you, so that His purposes will be accomplished on the earth. You received the promise of the Spirit. "Do you not know that your body is the temple of the Holy Spirit…and you are not your own? For you were bought at a price; therefore glorify God in your body…" (I Cor. 6:19, 20).

Jesus shed His blood on the cross to redeem you from the hand of Satan to bring you to the blessing, but the primary purpose in the New Testament is to wash you with His own precious blood so that the Spirit of God can fill you. He works in a clean place. He wants to use you, your body and all your earthly faculties, to reach this world.

John 16:13 "When He, the Spirit of truth, has come, He will guide you into all truth, for He will not speak of His own authority."

It is from God the Father's bosom that all plans come. What the Spirit hears the Father and the Son say, He'll transmit to you.

When you are born again, you can hear from God—even as a brand new Christian. "The Spirit Himself bears witness with our spirit that we are children of God" (Rom. 8:16).

When you make a decision for Christ, you know you're born again because the Holy Spirit inside you gives you an inward witness.

That inward witness will work in you, if you do what the Word says! The Word says, "as newborn babes, desire the pure milk of the word, that you may grow thereby" (I Peter 2:2).

YOU HAVE TO LEARN TO RECOGNIZE THE INNER PROMPTINGS OF THE SPIRIT. READ THE BIBLE. MEDITATE ON GOD'S WORD. PRAY IN THE SPIRIT. AND THEN DO WHAT SOME CALL "PRACTICING THE PRESENCE OF GOD."

Romans 8:14 says, "For as many as are led by the Spirit of God, these are the sons of God." That inward witness in your Spirit is like a green light or a red light. You're always listening. You should never go more than three days without an answer. If you've got a question that you want to ask Him, you yield yourself to Him. And you say, "Lord, I need to know about this." Then don't ask Him any more questions for about three days, just that one. And you stay in His presence. The inward witness is the primary way the Spirit leads. If the answer is yes, you have a soft, velvety feeling. If it's no, it's like a red light. You get in trouble when you override your spirit. The Spirit leads you and guides you so you won't make mistakes in your life.

Talk to God. Communion with the Holy Ghost is so wonderful. People live on the edge of having a nervous breakdown. But you can live in a high place with God. You'll have no more trouble with sin or doubt. Learn to cooperate with Him, and you will be able to avoid making mistakes. Live a life yielded to His plan. To hear from Him you have to do it His way. Miracles will follow when we live a holy life led by the Lord.

—Adapted from a message given at CFNI in Dallas.

Dr. Billye Brim is a Bible teacher. She founded Prayer Mountain in the Ozarks and the Migdal Arbel Prayer and Study Center in Israel. Dr. Brim is called to pray and enable prayer for an awakening to God for all nations.

Reprinted by permission: Christ for the Nations

CFNI, P.O. Box 769000, Dallas, TX 75376-9000, 800-933-2364

LESSON 6

OBEYING THE SPIRIT

MAIN PRINCIPLE

As we learn to obey the Holy Spirit, we will become more aware of how the Holy Spirit can minister through us.

TWELVE POINTS TO REMEMBER: HEARING THE VOICE OF GOD

by Loren Cunningham

If you know the Lord, you have already heard His voice—it is that inner leading that brought you to Him in the first place. Jesus always checked with His Father (John 8:26-29), and so should we. Hearing the voice of the heavenly Father is a basic right of every child of God. In this book we have tried to describe a few of many ways of fine-tuning this experience. The discoveries are never just theory. They come out of our own adventures:

1. Don't make guidance complicated. It's actually hard not to hear God if you really want to please and obey Him! If you stay humble, He promises to guide you (Prov. 16:9).

    Here are three simple steps that have helped us to hear God's voice:

    *   *Submit* to His lordship. Ask Him to help you silence your own thoughts and desires and the opinions of others that may be filling your mind (2 Cor. 10:5). Even though you have been given a good mind to use, right now you want to hear the thoughts of the Lord, who has the best mind (Prov. 3:5-6).

    *   *Resist* the enemy in case he is trying to deceive you at this moment. Use the authority that Jesus Christ has given you to silence the voice of the enemy (James 4:7; Eph. 6:10-20).

    *   *Expect* an answer. After asking the question that is on your mind, wait for Him to answer. Expect your loving heavenly Father to speak to you. He will (John 10:27; Ps 69:13; Exod. 33:11).

2. Allow God to speak to you in the way He chooses. Don't try to dictate to Him concerning the guidance methods you prefer. He is Lord—you are His servant (1 Sam. 3:9). Listen with a yielded heart; there is a direct link between yieldedness and hearing.

    God may choose to speak to you through His *Word*: This could come in your daily reading, or He could guide you to a particular verse (Ps. 119:105); through an *audible voice* (Exod. 3:4); through *dreams* (Matt. 2) and *visions* (Isa. 6:1, Rev. 1:12-17). But probably the most common of all means is through the quiet *inner voice* (Isa. 30:21).

3. Confess any unforgiven sin. A clean heart is necessary if you want to hear God (Ps. 66:18).

4. Use the Axhead Principle—a term coined from the story in 2 Kings 6. If you seem to have lost your way, go back to the last time you knew the sharp, cutting edge of God's voice. Then obey. The key question is, *Have you obeyed the last thing God told you to do?*

5. Get your own leading. God will use others to confirm your guidance, but you should also hear from Him directly. It can be dangerous to rely on others to get the word of the Lord for you (1 Kings 13).

6. Don't talk about your guidance until God gives you permission to do so. Sometimes this happens immediately; at other times, there is a delay. The main purpose of waiting is to avoid four pitfalls of guidance: (a) *pride,* because God has spoken something to you;

(b) *presumption,* by speaking before you have full understanding; (c) missing God's *timing and method;* (d) bringing *confusion* to others; they, too, need prepared hearts (Luke 9:36; Eccles. 3:7; Mark 5:19).

7. Use the Wise Men Principle. Just as the Three Wise Men individually followed the star and, in doing so, were all led to the same Christ, so God will often use two or more spiritually sensitive people to *confirm* what He is telling you (2 Cor. 13:1).

8. Beware of counterfeits. Have you ever heard of a counterfeit dollar bill? Yes, of course. But have you ever heard of a counterfeit paper bag? No. The reason is that the only things of value are worth counterfeiting.

   Satan has a counterfeit for everything of God that is possible for him to copy (Acts 8:9-11; Exod. 7:22). Counterfeit guidance comes, for example, through Ouija boards, séances, fortune-telling, and astrology (Lev. 20:6; 19:26; 2 Kings 21:6). The guidance of the Holy Spirit leads you closer to Jesus and into freedom. Satan's guidance leads you away from God into bondage.

   Once key test for true guidance: Does your leading follow principles of the Bible? The Holy Spirit never contradicts the Word of God.

9. Opposition of man is sometimes guidance from God (Acts 21:10-14). In our own story, we recognized much later that what seemed like blockage from our denomination was, in fact, God leading us into a broader scope of ministry. The important lesson here, again, is *yieldedness* to the Lord (Dan. 6:6-23; Acts 4:18-21). Rebellion is never of God, but sometimes He asks you to step away from your elders in a way that is not rebellion but a part of His plan. Trust that He will show your heart the difference.

10. Every follower of Jesus has a unique ministry (1 Cor. 12; 1 Pet. 4:10-11; Rom. 12; Eph. 4). The more you seek to hear God's voice in detail, the more effective you will be in your own calling. Guidance is not a game—it is serious business where we learn *what* God want us to do in ministry and *how* He wants us to do it. The will of God is doing and saying the right thing in the right place, with the right people, at the right time, and in the right sequence, under the right leadership, using the right method, with the right attitude of heart.

11. Practice hearing God's voice and it becomes easier. It's like picking up the phone and recognizing the voice of your best friend—you know his voice because you have heard it so much. Compare young Samuel with the older man Samuel (1 Sam. 3:4-7; 8:7-10; 12:11-18).

12. Relationship is the most important reason for hearing the voice of the Lord. God is not only infinite but also personal. If you don't have communication, you don't have a personal relationship with Him. True guidance, as Darlene pointed out, is getting closer to the Guide. We grow to know the Lord better as He speaks to us, and as we listen to Him and obey, we make His heart glad (Exod. 33:11; Matt. 7:24-27).

—Excerpted from pp. 200-203 of Loren Cunningham's *Is That Really You, God?* YWAM Publishing, P.O. Box 55787, Seattle, WA 98155.

YOUNG ADULT HEARING GOD'S VOICE
OBEYING THE SPIRIT

2 Chronicles 19 and 20 Study Help

Jehoshaphat was **afraid** because of the multitudes coming against his people. Earlier he had not heeded the warning of the prophet Micaiah to *not* go into battle with King Ahab and had almost lost his life **(2 Chronicles 18:16, 27, 31)**. This time Jehoshaphat was ready to listen and obey.

> **Question:** Have you experienced times when you knew you weren't supposed to do something and went ahead and did it?

1. Jehoshaphat proclaimed a fast and **inquired of the Lord.**

   Question: How many times have you asked the Lord for direction before making a decision in your life?

2. Jehoshaphat **prayed to God.** He acknowledged God's power and his own powerlessness. He **entreated God's mercy.** "We don't know what to do, but our eyes are upon you."

3. Jehoshaphat **heeded what the Spirit was saying** through the prophet Jahaziel.

   Question: Have you obeyed the Lord when he spoke to you about something in your life?

4. Jehoshaphat **waited** for the proper time. **"Tomorrow march down against them."**

   Question: Timing is so important. Have you ever pushed ahead before God wanted you to? If so, what were the results?

5. Jehoshaphat told the people to have **faith in the Lord** and **listen to God's prophets.**

   Faith was needed in order to follow through on the simple directions. God did not give the whole picture.

6. Jehoshaphat consulted the people and he thought they had God's favor, protection and promised victory.

7. He was **obedient** and carried out his only "plan"—to praise God and send singers!

The Results:

1. God dealt with the problem and gave them **victory!**

2. **God was glorified** as they **praised God with much joy.**

3. God gave Judah **peace** and **rest** in the Lord.

> **Question:** When you are obedient to the leading of the Holy Spirit, what are the results in your life? Is there joy, peace or rest?

LESSON 7

WHAT KEEPS US FROM HEARING GOD´S VOICE?

MAIN PRINCIPLE

*As we seek to hear God's voice more clearly, we will need
to keep our hearts yielded toward the Lord. Sin in our
life acts as a barrier to communication with God.*

YOUNG ADULT HEARING GOD'S VOICE
WHAT KEEPS US FROM HEARING?

These scriptures either:

   a) show how a specific issue acts as a hindrance to hearing God,
   b) contain a promise of hearing God when you deal with that issue, or
   c) provide help in overcoming the hindrance.

Scriptures

1. Not spending time with the Lord—in prayer, the Word and worship:
   Isaiah 30:21
   James 1:5
   2 Timothy 3:16–17
   Psalm 119:105
   Psalm 24:3, 5

2. Walking in unforgiveness:
   Mark 11:25
   Matthew 18:21–22
   Colossians 3:13
   Luke 6:35, 37

3. Unconfessed sin:
   Romans 12:1–2
   James 1:21, 25
   1 John 1:9
   Psalm 51:2

4. Unbelief:
   James 1:5–7
   Romans 10:17
   Proverbs 3:5–6
   Jeremiah 33:3

5. Fear:
   2 Timothy 1:7
   Romans 8:15–16
   Isaiah 54:17
   Psalm 25:12, 14

6. Lack of knowledge:
   Hosea 4:6

7. Not being truly born again or filled with the Spirit:
   John 3:1–21   **John 8:47**
   Romans 10:9–13   **Acts 1 and 2**

FORGIVING MY FATHER

by Josh McDowell

JOSH MCDOWELL GREW UP HATING HIS FATHER, THE TOWN ALCOHOLIC.
THEN SOMETHING CHANGED.

I grew up on a dairy farm near Union City, Michigan. My older brothers and sisters had left home by the time I was in junior high school, so it was just me and my parents on the farm. I loved my mother, but I despised my father more than anyone else in the world. He was the town alcoholic, and everybody knew it. My friends would make jokes about my father being downtown, drunk. They didn't think it bothered me. I was laughing on the outside, but crying on the inside.

At one end–of–the–year school outing, my class had a picnic at our farm. Everyone was having a good time until my dad drove into the driveway. The old pickup swerved back and forth, kicking up clouds of dust as Dad drove toward the barn. He barely avoided hitting a tree, a fence and my pet collie. As he stopped the pickup and got out, he nearly fell, then staggered toward the house. When the kids saw he was intoxicated, they laughed and joked.

I hated my father for the embarrassment and shame his alcoholism caused my family. I also resented what it caused him to do to my mother. I'd go out in the barn and see my mother beaten so badly she couldn't get up, lying in the manure behind the cows. When we had friends over, I would take my father out, tie him up in the barn and park the car up around the silo. We would tell our friends that he'd had to go somewhere.

I often resorted to extreme means in dealing with my dad. One time I tied him so that his feet were trussed with a rope that was noosed around his neck, hoping that he would kick his legs trying to get free and choke himself.

One time I came home and found my mother crying because of Dad's drinking and abuse. I wrestled Dad into the bathroom and stuck his head in the toilet to sober him up. I kept pushing his head up and down in the water, and if the bowl had been deeper and I hadn't splashed most of the water out, I probably would have drowned him. Usually we just swept incidents like this under the rug and never dealt with them.

About two months before I graduated from high school, I came home from a date and heard my mother crying profusely. That shook me up. I said, "Mom, what's wrong?"

"I can't take it anymore," she said. "Your father has broken my heart, and I've lost the will to live. All I want to do is live until you graduate, and then I just want to die."

Two months later I graduated, and the next Friday my mother died. Don't tell me you can't die of a broken heart, because my mother did, and my father was the one who broke it.

After her funeral I enrolled at Kellogg College in Battle Creek, Michigan, and met some people who were Christians. My mother had instilled in me a respect for God, but as I got older, I saw religion as just being rituals that had no effect on anything. There was something different about these people, however. One day they challenged me to intellectually examine the claims of Jesus Christ.

After several months of studying the evidence about Him, I came to the conclusion that Jesus must have been who He claimed to be. I thanked Him for dying on the cross for me, confessed the things in my life that weren't pleasing to Him, and asked Him to come into my heart and take control of me.

After I prayed, I began to see that my life was changed. While the results were not as obvious to others, there was one way I knew a supernatural event had occurred: My hatred for my father had miraculously melted.

I had confessed to God my feelings for my dad, asked God to forgive me, and prayed that I could forgive. And it happened as quickly as I asked.

No longer was my dad a drunk to be hated. Now I saw him as a man who had helped give me life. I called him and told him two things I had never told him before: "Dad, I've become a Christian, and . . . I love you."

Shortly after that, I was in a serious car accident. My neck was in traction, and I was taken home to recover. My dad welcomed me home. A few days later, he came into my room crying. It was the first time I had ever seen him cry. "You're different now, Josh," he said. "You don't act like you hate me anymore."

"I don't," I replied softly. Looking him in the eyes, I added, "I love you." And I meant it.

"But how . . . how can you love a father like me?" he stammered.

"Last year I couldn't," I explained. "And six months ago, I despised you." I explained to him how to ask God for forgiveness and how to receive Christ into his life.

"Son," he said, "if God will work in my life the way He's worked in yours, to let you love someone the likes of me, then I want to give Him the opportunity."

Right there my father prayed with me. It was one of the greatest thrills of my life. His conversion was so dramatic—I had never seen one like it before and have never seen one like it since. He touched alcohol only once after that; he got it to his lips and that was all. He didn't need it anymore.

But due to more than 40 years of drinking, his body had been damaged too much. About 14 months later, my father died. During that 14–month period, scores of people in my hometown and the surrounding areas committed their lives to Christ because of the changed life of the town alcoholic, my father. He also took time to establish with me the kind of father role that I want to give to my son.

My dad's life was brand new those last 14 months. His relationship with me and with God were both reconciled. Jesus Christ is a peacemaker.

—Josh McDowell is a Christian apologist, evangelist and writer, who has been closely affiliated with Campus Crusade for Christ. In his role as a popular apologist, McDowell has spoken across the United States and in many other nations.

Reprinted by permission: Worldwide Challenge

LESSON 8

DIFFERENT WAYS GOD SPEAKS—
INNER KNOWING

MAIN PRINCIPLE

*The inner knowing is a common way God leads us. It can
take the form of a "knowing that you know," a holy hunch,
a sudden uneasiness, a sense of peace or a caution.*

YOUNG ADULT HEARING GOD'S VOICE
INNER KNOWING

The inner knowing is a common way that God speaks to His children.

The inner knowing can be:

    1. An intuition, a "knowing that you know" something, a holy hunch.

    2. A calm or peace that indicates that you have God's "go-ahead."

    3. An uneasiness or a hesitation that should cause you to stop and reassess the situation.

    4. A caution—the signal to wait.

As the Scriptures are read, look for the different ways God provides guidance. Especially note examples of the inner knowing.

You may note these in the spaces above or list them below.

—Some concepts in this Study Help came from Kenneth Hagin's *How You Can Be Led By The Spirit Of God.*

DEATH CAMP REVISITED

by Corrie ten Boom

CORRIE TEN BOOM'S FACE–TO–FACE "REUNION" WITH A CONCENTRATION CAMP GUARD CHALLENGED HER CAPACITY TO FORGIVE.

It was in a church in Munich that I saw him—a balding, heavyset man in a gray overcoat, a brown felt hat clutched between his hands. People were filing out of the basement room where I had just spoken, moving along the rows of wooden chairs to the door at the rear. It was 1947 and I had come from Holland to defeated Germany with the message that God forgives.

It was the truth they needed most to hear in that bitter, bombed–out land, and I gave them my favorite mental picture. Maybe because the sea is never far from a Hollander's mind, I liked to think that that's where forgiven sins were thrown. "When we confess our sins," I said, "God casts them into the deepest ocean, gone forever. And even though I cannot find a Scripture for it, I believe God then places a sign out there that says, 'No Fishing Allowed.' "

The solemn faces stared back at me, not quite daring to believe. There were never questions after a talk in Germany in 1947. People stood up in silence, in silence collected their wraps, in silence left the room.

And that's when I saw him, working his way forward against the others. One moment I saw the overcoat and the brown hat; the next, a blue uniform and a visored cap with its skull and crossbones. It came back with a rush: the huge room with its harsh overhead lights; the pathetic pile of dresses and shoes in the center of the floor; the shame of walking naked past this man. I could see my sister's frail form ahead of me, ribs sharp beneath the parchment skin.

The place was Ravensbruck, and the man who was making his way forward had been a guard.

Now he was in front of me, hand thrust out: "A fine message, *Fraulein*! How good it is to know that, as you say, all our sins are at the bottom of the sea!"

And I, who had spoken so glibly of forgiveness, fumbled in my pocketbook rather than take that hand. He would not remember me, of course—how could he remember one prisoner among those thousands of women?

But I remembered him and the leather crop swinging from his belt. I was face to face with one of my captors, and my blood seemed to freeze.

"You mentioned Ravensbruck in your talk," he was saying. "I was a guard there." No, he did not remember me.

"But since that time," he went on, "I have become a Christian. I know that God has forgiven me for the cruel things I did there, but I would like to hear it from your lips as well. *Fraulein*,"—again the hand came out—"will you forgive me?"

And I stood there—I whose sins had to be forgiven again and again—and could not forgive. Even as the angry, vengeful thoughts boiled through me, I saw the sin of them. Jesus Christ had died for this man; was I going to ask for more? *Lord Jesus*, I prayed, *forgive me and help me to forgive him*.

For I had to do it—I knew that. The message that God forgives has a prior condition: that we forgive those who have injured us. "If you do not forgive men their trespasses," Jesus says, "neither will your Father in heaven forgive your trespasses."

And still I stood there with the coldness clutching my heart. But forgiveness is not an emotion—I knew that too. Forgiveness is an act of the will, and the will can function regardless of the temperature of the heart. *Jesus, help me!* I prayed silently. *I can lift my hand. I can do that much. You supply the feeling.*

And so woodenly, mechanically, I thrust my hand into the one stretched out to me. And as I did, an incredible thing took place. The current started in my shoulder, raced down my arm, sprang into our joined hands. And then this healing warmth seemed to flood my whole being, bringing tears to my eyes.

"I forgive you, brother!" I cried. "With all my heart."

And so I discovered that it is not on our forgiveness any more than on our goodness that the world's healing hinges, but on His. When He tells us to love our enemies, He gives, along with the command, the love itself.

For a long moment we grasped each other's hands, the former guard and the former prisoner. I had never known God's love so intensely as I did then. But even so, I realized it was not my love. I had tried and did not have the power. It was the power of the Holy Spirit.

—Adapted from *The Hiding Place*, Corrie ten Boom with John and Elizabeth Sherrill, Chappaqua, N.Y.: Chosen Books Inc.; and *Tramp for the Lord*, Corrie ten Boom with Jamie Buckingham © 1974, Fleming H. Revell, a division of Baker Book House.

Corrie ten Boom (1892-1983) was born in the Netherlands. She and her family hid Jews from the Nazis during World War II.

Reprinted by permission: Worldwide Challenge

LESSON 9

DIFFERENT WAYS GOD SPEAKS— INNER VOICE

MAIN PRINCIPLE

God can communicate with us through the inner voice, which is quiet guidance with words. This still, small voice is the gentle whisper of the Holy Spirit in our spirit.

WHEN GOD SAYS, 'WAIT'

by Iverna Tompkins

WE ALWAYS WANT GOD TO MOVE
ACCORDING TO OUR TIMETABLE,
YET HIS WORK SEEMS SLOW AND
TEDIOUS. THAT'S BECAUSE OUR
FATHER HAS MORE PLANNED FOR
US THAN WE CAN EVER IMAGINE.

One of the most exciting revelations we can have as Christians is the understanding that God has a specific plan for us. The Scriptures clearly tell us that God fashioned each one of us with a goal in mind. We are not mere accidents, afterthoughts or the result of a spark in our parent's eyes: We were created for a purpose!

Knowing this gives meaning to our existence, influences the choices we make, and provides motivation for our Christian walk. But it can also cause us to become impatient whenever we seem to be doing things that are unrelated to our purpose.

God created me to be a preacher. But I was almost 30 years old before I began preaching regularly. Before that, I was involved in the business world, social work and counseling. If I had known then what I would be doing today, I am sure I would have fussed and fretted about wasting my time. Now I can see that everything I have done has given me a much richer and broader background to relate to people.

During my younger years I worked as a supervisor in a country home for wayward girls. These girls were tough; many were gang members. But I always knew how to handle them, even when the other counselors didn't.

Staff members would ask, "How did you know what to do?"

"You're not going to accept what I say," I'd answer, "but the Lord showed me what to do."

My Christian friends thought I was right where God wanted me to be. But I was dissatisfied. I wasn't allowed to talk about the Lord with the girls, and deep inside me was a sense that *this is good—but it's not what I have been purposed for.*

One night, I attended a special meeting at a local church and was surprised when the pastor confronted me. "Why are you wasting your life on things that are not eternal?" she demanded.

At first I thought the Lord was telling me through this pastor to leave my job. But then the Holy Spirit gave me God's answer to her question: "Because these things have an eternal purpose." Although I did not see it at the time, something was taking place in me as I cared for those girls that was preparing me for a later time of ministry.

THE BEST OCCUPATION

God uses placements to help us learn what He wants us to learn, so we can be prepared to fulfill our purpose. Even when we do not understand why He makes us stay in a certain place or job or situation, or why He moves us on, we can be assured that He is working all things for our good according to His eternal plan (see Rom. 8:28).

Jesus trusted the Father to always place Him right where He wanted Him, uncomfortable as the situation might be. The Scriptures tell us that Jesus learned obedience from what He suffered (see Heb. 5:8). He could have called 10,000 angels to stop His persecutors when their actions were leading to His death. But He didn't—because He had learned obedience through years of doing whatever God asked Him to do.

August 1996, Charisma

We know that Jesus spent His early years learning to become a carpenter. I imagine He must have thought at least once, "Why am I here at home right now instead of out there with the people? I have so little time." Yet He submitted to God's plan.

From God's perspective, it isn't our occupation that matters, it's what we're learning that counts. He says, "Are you learning love, joy, peace, patience, kindness, goodness, faith, gentleness and self-control? Great! If not, I'll move you to a more intense placement where you will."

Some of us will be led to get advanced college degrees. Some will be led to be teachers, mechanics, construction workers, accountants, secretaries and so on. Will we use our degrees or our job skills in eternity? I don't know. But I know these things can open doors for us to accomplish the purpose of God on earth.

Sometimes we say to God, in effect: "Lord, I trust You, but it would certainly help if You'd tell me why I'm here. Please just explain what You're doing, why, when and how much it will cost."

But God has little sympathy for our desire to know His plans in advance. He replies: "That isn't the way I work. That's the way man works."

DIFFICULT PLACEMENTS

God used placements in David's life to develop character and prepare him for the day he would be king. As a boy, he was a shepherd. It was demanding and a monotonous job, the least desirable of all the chores in a family.

But David's experiences while protecting the sheep helped him to become brave, a characteristic he would need to face Goliath. The periods he spent tending sheep gave him the opportunity to play the harp and fellowship with God, providing a skill and an anointing that he would need to minister to King Saul.

The greatest test for David came when Saul became jealous and determined to destroy him. David had to flee from Israel—the very nation God had anointed him to lead. He moved from hiding place to hiding place, learning to trust God because he had nowhere else to turn.

David had to wait for the throne, but not because King Saul was still alive. God could have killed Saul in a second. But because David still required much preparation for his placement, God left Saul on the throne and used him to speed up the process of David's maturation.

> BUT GOD HAS LITTLE SYMPATHY FOR OUR DESIRE TO KNOW HIS PLANS IN ADVANCE.

The prophet Samuel was the first person to learn that God had removed Saul's authority to be king of Israel. First, God told Samuel, "Anoint Saul." Then God said, in essence, "Defrock him!"

Samuel was not happy about this latter assignment. In the same way, many of us are not happy about ending something God led us to begin. If God says "Now start this," we rarely want to hear Him say, "Now stop it."

It is so easy to start out following God's placement but then go beyond it when we see success. I know of one church that mistakenly came into being when God's directive to a small group of Christians was simply to have neighbors in for coffee. God never mandated a new church to come forth.

We can find it difficult to believe that God would not want a successful home ministry to get bigger and become a new church. We find it especially hard when it is our successful home ministry!

At times, we try to usurp God's role in reassigning individuals to new placements. When a primary Sunday school class grows numerically and spiritually because there's an anointing on the teacher, we promptly give him or her more responsibility. If the same thing happens in the new placement, then we promote the individual again.

The anointed primary teacher is promoted from position to position, until a level is reached where he or she is unable to function at all. Such people don't lose their anointing; they allow others to help them misplace it!

If we can learn that God's beginnings and endings don't have to make sense to us, then God can commit to us a lot of beginnings. He can rely on us not to mistake placement as a home group leader for a call to pastor a church. He can depend on us to stop a work when He tells us to.

ACCEPTING RE-PLACEMENT

At one point in his life when David was running from King Saul, he escaped to the cave of Adullam, where he was joined by his brothers and his father's household, as well as 400 other men. After arranging to leave his parents with the king of Moab, David set up camp in a "stronghold" (1 Sam. 22:4).

David and his men were safe. His parents were secure in Moab. What was there to motivate him to move on?

When we get into a safe place (sometimes it's a church), we don't worry about the enemy coming from the north, south, east or west. We let the guards (church leaders) watch for us. If we have food (the pastor feeding the flock), water (the washing of the Word) and friends, we're really not inclined to allow God to change our placement.

I had a comfortable stronghold where I stayed for nine years—the wonderful church where my brother Judson Cornwall and I pastored together. I liked being under Judson's protection. If people in the congregation had an objection to women ministers, I would send them to his office, and when he got through with them they had no more complaints. I loved living there, and had no intention of ever leaving.

Then God said, "I want to move you out to the body of Christ." I wasn't willing to hear that word. Everything was too wonderful right where I was. Then God spoke the same word to Judson: "I want you to go to the body of Christ." Judson, who was not stubborn like his sister, said: "Wonderful, Lord. Today or tomorrow?" And he started traveling, leaving me with the church.

"I can do this," I said to myself, and I pastored in his absence. I continued feeling comfortable there until Judson began to stay away for longer and longer periods of time. He'd come home in the middle of the week, and then he'd be gone again. Finally, it seemed that he was never at the church anymore.

"Okay, I'll handle things," I said, and I began to dig in. But God had other plans. After a series of difficult events, I made a decision to resign.

Despite God's earlier call, I felt unworthy to serve the Lord anywhere else. Then I was singled out at a meeting and a prophetic minister reiterated: "The Lord is going to send you to the whole body of Christ.

With the pressure of God's previous words to me already bearing down on my stiff neck, I could no longer ignore the voice of God when the prophet repeated His message.

PREPARING FOR CORONATION

Placement is something we all must deal with every moment of our lives. God uses our placements to develop the fruit of the Spirit in our lives—and these fruits prepare us for future placements.

David had to wait to become king because God was getting him ready. We need to be made ready, as well. Even after we are called and anointed, we must be prepared for our roles before God can appoint us.

We needn't be anxious. The key to contentment during our periods of preparation is focusing on what God wants us to do—and what He wants to do in us—while we're waiting. We can prepare for our coronation

August 1996, Charisma

with patience and great joy. It will come in God's time.

—Adapted from *All in God's Time* by Iverna Tompkins, copyright 1996. Published by Creation House. Used by permission.

Iverna Tompkins served as a Pentecostal pastor during the charismatic movement of the 1960s and 1970s. Through her teaching and preaching ministry, Dr. Tompkins shares the message of an ever-deepening relationship with Jesus and trains leaders in the body of Christ.

Reprinted by permission: Charisma Magazine and Strang Communications

LESSON 10

DIFFERENT WAYS GOD SPEAKS— AUTHORITATIVE VOICE OF THE HOLY SPIRIT

MAIN PRINCIPLE

The Holy Spirit can speak to believers with words that seem to us to be audible to those around us. What He says will never contradict Scripture.

DIFFERENT WAYS GOD SPEAKS—AUTHORITATIVE VOICE OF THE HOLY SPIRIT

Article: *Twelve Points To Remember*, Points 9 and 10 (Refer to Lesson 6 pages 47-48)

LESSON 11

OTHER MANIFESTATIONS
OF THE HOLY SPIRIT

MAIN PRINCIPLE

*God can communicate with us through dreams,
visions and other manifestations of the Holy Spirit.*

YOUNG ADULT HEARING GOD'S VOICE
REVIEW OF HEARING GOD'S VOICE

1. **Inner Knowing (knowing that you know, holy hunch, a signal to stop, go ahead or wait)**

   a. Romans 8:14-17

   b. Acts 16:6-7

2. **Inner Voice (still small voice)**

   a. 1 Kings 19:12

   b. Isaiah 30:21

   c. Acts 8:29

   d. Acts 10:19-20

3. **Authoritative Voice**

   a. Acts 9:15-16

   b. 1 Samuel 3

4. **Visions and Dreams**

   a. Acts 9:10-16

   b. 1 Samuel 3:1-15

   c. Acts 10:1-16

   d. Daniel 2:19

   e. Numbers 12:6

   f. Joel 2:27-28

5. **Other Manifestations of the Operation of the Holy Spirit**

   a. **The Spiritual Gifts of the Holy Spirit**

      1 Corinthians 12:7-11

b. **Falling**

   John 18:2-6

   Acts 9:3-8

   Revelation 1:17

c. **Dove**

   Matthew 3:16

d. **Wind**

   Acts 2:2

e. **Fire**

   Isaiah 6:4-7

   Acts 2:3

   Exodus 3:2

   Exodus 13:21-22

f. **Cloud / Glory**

   2 Chronicles 5:13-14

   Exodus 40:34-35

   Revelation 15:8

g. **Fragrance**

   2 Corinthians 2:14-15

   Exodus 30:22-25

h. **Angels**

   Acts 10:3-7

   Genesis 28:12

HEARING GOD'S VOICE

by Don WIlliams

> "CHURCHES AND SUCCESS MAY COME AND GO, BUT IN THAT MOMENT I WAS AT HOME, HELD IN THE PALM OF GOD'S HAND."

I sat alone in the early morning darkness, unemployed and confused about the future. Eight years of building a church and leading it into renewal now lay behind me. Politics at the highest level of leadership had resulted in my ouster as pastor, much to the shock of the congregation and myself.

Rather than fighting for my position, however, I knew that the Lord wanted me to go home and be quiet and wait. Nevertheless, the frustration was building. With the passing of several months, time and money seemed to be running out.

The stillness enveloped me as I sat before my desk and began praying. I shook off the chill, and my petitions gained force. I cried out audibly, "Lord, what do you want me to do?" The tears began to wash my cheeks and I now trailed off... "Lord, what do you want? Lord...." Suddenly, in the intense quiet, a voice spoke within me, "I want you."

Do you get it? The mighty King, Yahweh, God over all, wanted, as my earthly father would say, "Donny Boy." I was in his heart. Churches and success may come and go, but in that moment I was at home, held in the palm of his hand.

QUESTIONS

Reflecting on this incident, you may well ask, "How did you know that this was the voice of God?" Be assured that I too have asked this question. Many sincere Christians ask that question, and add many more objections: "We do not hear God's voice in this way today." And they add, "If God speaks directly and personally to us, how can we be certain that it is him?" "Isn't there the danger that this is our own voice now disguised as divine?" Or, darker still, they would wonder if this was the devil's whisper.

My experience raises many other questions: "If we do admit that God speaks directly, doesn't this undermine the absolute authority of the Bible?" "How can we reconcile the living Word of God with the written Word of God?" "Isn't the canon of Scripture compromised if God speaks directly to us today?" "What would prevent us from logically and theologically taking such words and binding them into our Bibles as new revelation?" I'll address these questions in the remainder of this article.

To begin with, God's written Word is needed for at least two reasons. First of all, the Bible reveals how God speaks and thus prepares me to hear his living word. Second of all, the Bible both tests and often provides the content for that word. I'll look at each of these topics in order.

> IS THERE A VERSE IN WHICH HE SAYS, "AFTER THE SCRIPTURES ARE COMPLETE, I WILL NOT SPEAK THROUGH VISIONS, ANGELS, PROPHESIES, OR LIVING WORDS ANYMORE TO YOU?"

VISIONS AND DREAMS

As an evangelical Christian, I believe that the Bible is the fully inspired Word of God, the only rule of

IN INSISTING THAT WE CAN HEAR THE LIVING VOICE OF GOD TODAY, WE ARE RESTORING TO THE EXPERIENCE OF THE CONTEMPORARY CHURCH ALL THAT THE BIBLE REVEALS CONCERNING HOW HE SPEAKS.

faith and practice. Thus, it establishes the norms for both what we believe and how we are to practice that belief. But when we read the Bible, we begin to see that God is revealed as the living God who, in contrast to the dumb idols, speaks to his people. This is a part of his uniqueness as God, and a necessary part of what it means to be able to have a personal relationship with him through the Lord Jesus Christ.

Again and again, we are exhorted in the Scriptures to "Hear the word of the Lord!" But how does this word come to us? All evangelicals would agree that the word comes through the Bible. For this reason, the great hallmark of evangelicalism is preaching and teaching.

When the Pope travels he takes his altar and says mass, but when Billy Graham travels he takes his pulpit and preaches the message of the Book. So far so good. The rub comes now, however, when we discover in the Bible that the living God speaks directly to his people in many other ways apart from reading through the Bible itself.

For example, in the Book of Acts alone, along with teaching and preaching, God speaks through visions, dreams, prophetic words, audible and inaudible voices, and angelic messengers. With the closing of the canon of Scripture, does God also close down these various means of his communications? And if he does, can we prove this from the Bible itself? Is there a verse in which he says, "After the Scriptures are complete, I will not speak through visions, angels, prophecies, or living words anymore to you"? Of course not! In fact, God promises to continue to be so personal to his people that they will actually hear his voice (Acts 2:16-21; cf. Joel 2:28-32). Thus, to restrict the voice of God to the written Word alone is to become functionally unbiblical.

The absence of the living word returns us to that period of Israel's history when, according to the Rabbis (due to God's judgment), the Holy Spirit had departed, leaving God's people with only the Book to study. This view may create a generation of scribes, but it will never create a generation of friends of God who are becoming intimate with his heart.

In insisting that we can hear the living voice of God today, we are restoring to the experience of the contemporary church all that the Bible reveals concerning how he speaks. The Bible, however, not only shows us how God speaks, it also both tests that speech and often provides its content. To this we now turn.

TESTING

Since the Bible is our only absolute revelation, all other revealed words must meet the measure of this Word. For example, when the Lord said to me, "I want you," how can I know that this was he? While I believe that as his sheep, I know his voice (John 10:3) and that the Holy Spirit witnesses that voice to my spirit (Rom. 8:16; 1 John 2:27), I still can be misled by my own needs or even the seductions of Satan, disguising himself as an angel of light (2 Cor. 11:14) and become cultic. Therefore, the living word must be tested by the written Word.

In this case, God did not answer my vocational plea directly. His surprising response gave me confidence that I did not merely make up his voice out of my own need for direction. Rather than showing me what he wanted me to do, he took me deeper into his heart to confront the real issue. He was concerned about who I am; his interest was my relationship with him. In saying that he wanted me, the Lord affirmed that he is personal, that I am the object of his love, and that in my pain and loss I am still valuable to him.

Moreover, this living word was completely consistent with the written Word. It added no new revelation, but it gave me personal reassurance like a shaft of light in the midst of my darkness. Here then this living word passed the light of Scripture clearly and easily.

I hasten to say that God could have responded to my plea ("What do you want me to do?") with, "Go to Duluth." This direct answer would have been harder to test biblically. Nevertheless, the Book of Acts witnesses to such concrete guidance (Acts 16:9), so there is scriptural precedent for such a word.

At the same time, in order for me to have absolute assurance that I should go to Duluth, I believe that such a directive would best be confirmed by other means. These would include supporting Scriptures, devotionally received, pointing in that direction; similar words given to others on my behalf; God's assurance to my wife that we should make such a move; circumstances encouraging us to go there; and the affirmation of those who are in spiritual authority over me. I would also add to these points an honest examination of my motives for such a move, granting me a sense of peace.

CONTENT

Furthermore, God's written Word not only provides the test for his living words to us, it also often provides the content as well. As we immerse our lives more and more in the Bible, its message determines our thought patterns and responses.

Jesus described this as "abiding" in his Word (John 8:31). Thus, we will find our prayers laced with scriptural phrases and our thoughts drawn to biblical passages. Verses will pursue us and surface in our conversation, and, when God speaks his living word to us it will often take biblical form as well. As we have access to the written Word, the Spirit will use that Word in addressing us in return.

CLOSED CANON?

In advocating our hearing the living word of God today, are we in danger of adding to the Bible itself? Does the concept of the living word invalidate the closing of the canon? (By "closed canon" I mean that the Bible is complete and no new books will be added.) The answer to this fear is simply, "No, the idea of the living word does not mean the Bible can be added to."

As we have already suggested, welcoming the living word of God into our hearts and our churches actually upholds the canon, making it more functional in our lives. What value is there for an orthodox view of the Bible that denies its practical application to the way we live? If God reveals that he speaks today through his living voice then we must be ready and willing to hear that voice.

Jesus only calls us wise if we both hear his word and do it (Matt. 7:24). It is the doers of the word who will not be self-deceived (James 1:22).

At the same time, the reason that we do not add God's current, living words to the canon of Scripture is clear. The fullness of God's revelation for this age has been given in his Son. As Paul tells the Colossians, "For in him [Christ] all the fullness of Deity dwells in bodily form, and in him you have been made complete..." (Col. 2: 9-10, NAS).

Moreover, the authorities for this revelation are the apostles who were eyewitnesses to his ministry and resurrection and who guarantee the authenticity of the New Testament. God's living words will bring personal conviction, assurance, and direction to us and to our churches. They may even bring a specific sense of what God is doing in our moment of history. However, they will never bring new, substantial truth and those who make this claim are either deluded or heretical.

In the early morning darkness when God said, "I want you," the lights went on in my heart. With a closer, more intimate walk with him, I entered into a new time of hearing his voice. Prayer in the "secret place" became not only a discipline but also a joy. And the future that the Lord had for me, beyond my present pain, began to unfold clearly.

IN THE EARLY MORNING DARKNESS WHEN GOD SAID, "I WANT YOU," THE LIGHTS WENT ON IN MY HEART.

With David I can witness, "I sought the Lord, and he answered me" (Ps. 34:4). Isn't that what it´s all about?

—Don Williams has served as pastor of the Coast Vineyard Christian Fellowship in La Jolla, California.

Reprinted by permission: Equipping the Saints

LESSON 12

"GO TELL!"

MAIN PRINCIPLE

As we remember what Jesus has done for us, we renew our determination to love and follow Him. As we recognize the gift of God within us, we are prepared to go out into the world and bring the good news of reconciliation with God the Father through Jesus by the power of the Holy Spirit.

ARTICLE

THE NEW BREED OF WORLD CHANGERS

by Nevers Mumba

God is raising up a new breed of world changers. History reveals that the world's system openly defies the authority and wisdom of God. In order for change to come, God is calling for a new breed of leadership to arise within the body of Christ!

This new breed is unwilling to compromise. It goes back to the basics, preaching the blood of Jesus, the cross, salvation, redemption and the baptism of the Holy Spirit—messages that are uncommon today. To become one of the new breed, you must be willing to pay the price. You must be different.

God confronted the young man, Jeremiah, saying "'Before I formed you in the womb I knew you; before you were born I sanctified you; I ordained you a prophet to the nations.' Then said I: 'Ah, LORD GOD! Behold, I cannot speak, for I am a youth.' But the LORD said to me: 'Do not say, "I am a youth," for you shall go to all to whom I send you; and whatever I command you, you shall speak. Do not be afraid of their faces, for I am with you to deliver you,' says the LORD. Then the LORD put forth His hand and touched my mouth, and the LORD said to me: 'Behold, I have put My words in your mouth. See, I have this day set you over the nations and over the kingdoms, to root out and to pull down, to destroy and to throw down, to build and to plant'" (Jer. 1:5-10).

I asked the Lord why He gave Jeremiah such a mighty introduction. I believe God was trying to identify Jeremiah not just as an ordinary prophet, but as a man marked by God to influence a generation. The life of every person called and anointed of God to change the world is also marked. It's not what people say about you or how weak you feel that counts. Your life is marked by God, and because of that, you are somebody. God is not in the business of wasting material. He has a purpose for your life which you need to discover, sharpen and fulfill if you are going to change your world.

There are three important qualities of this new breed of world changers. The first one is that they have information and share it with others. They know who they are in God. They know their mission and their message. One of the major problems facing our generation is that we are insecure about ourselves. We don't know what God can do in our lives. We don't recognize that God has called us by name, so we are full of apologies. But this breed of world changers knows who they are in Christ and preaches the basics of the Word of God.

It is not high-powered, high-voltage preaching that will change nations; it is people who are willing to preach the basics. Just preach the blood. Preach that Jesus died on the cross and that He's coming back again. Preach the fact that there is a future for those who know God and there is hope for those who follow Him. We have tried to improve on the Word of God by sugarcoating our message, and the power of God was withdrawn from us. It's not eloquence that reaches a nation; it's the simplicity of the power of the Gospel. There's only one message that gives hope to a lost generation: the message of our Lord Jesus Christ!

The quality of this new breed is that they are bold and uncompromising. The Bible says, "The righteous are bold as a lion" (Prov. 28:1). It doesn't matter how well you preach; if there is a lack of integrity in your life, your ministry is a big zero. If you lack integrity, there is no power. You may succeed for a few months, or even years; but in the end, your ministry will fold up. Your authority with God will equal your walk with God. If you walk right, miracles will happen because there is power in holiness.

One way this new breed walks right is by being unwilling to compromise. A deadly word in our generation today is compromise. Compromise is everywhere. "To compromise" means "to make a deal, to meet half way." We're living in a generation where many preachers are saying, "I don't want to offend anybody." But wisdom that brings that kind of compromise is not true wisdom— it's foolishness.

A spirit of humanism has entered the Church. Jesus called Herod a fox. He said, "Go, tell that fox..." (Lk. 13:32). Is this wisdom? Not earthly wisdom. Earthly wisdom would have said, "Go and tell his dignified excellency…" When animals were being sold and money was being changed in the temple, Jesus got a whip and began to overturn tables. He didn't go to the temple and say, "Let me find a wise way of communicating," God's wisdom is different than earthly wisdom—it is without compromise. God is looking for those who are willing to go against the tide of their day and say, "No!" when the world says, "Yes! Yes!" and say "Yes!" when the world says "No!"

It is costly to be uncompromising. Going against the crowd is much harder than going along with it. It's easier to come down a mountain than it is to go up. But the new generation of believers and leaders of the Church are going to be bold and uncompromising.

The third quality of this new breed is that they will be unpopular. Anybody in this lost generation who stands for truth must be willing to face persecution daily. If you preach the basics of the Word of God, the world will rise up against you. God gave Jeremiah a strong and uncompromising message to preach. It was an unpopular message.

Many times I have prayed, "God, deliver me from this message! Give me a good message! I have enough enemies!" But God keeps saying to me, "The generation in which you live is a generation that is out-of-joint." To place our generation back "in-joint," it's going to take a new breed of leadership within the church.

> IN ORDER FOR CHANGE TO COME, GOD IS CALLING FOR A NEW BREED OF LEADERSHIP TO ARISE WITHIN THE BODY OF CHRIST! THIS NEW BREED IS UNWILLING TO COMPROMISE.

Thank God for Stephen in the book of Acts, who stood up and challenged the Jewish leaders: "You stiff-necked and uncircumcised in heart and ears! Which of the prophets did your fathers persecute?" (Acts 7:51,52). Even though he spoke the truth, saying that cost him his life.

However, the good news is that when you stand up for Jesus, He will stand up for you! As Stephen was being stoned to death, he saw Jesus standing at the right hand of the Father. Jesus is now sitting on the right hand of God. But on that day, Stephen saw Him stand up and say, "Come on home, you great hero, for you have run a faithful race and you've completed your course." When you stand up for God in a generation that opposes Him, God is going to stand up for you!

The three Hebrew children—Shadrach, Meshach, and Abed-Nego— were challenged by Nebuchadnezzar to bow before the image. They were asked to compromise their faith in the only true God. Today we, too, are being told, "Compromise with what's happening in the Church and in the world today and everything's going to be alright. But if you decide to be different, we're going to burn you." The three Hebrew children chose to burn rather than bow.

Sometimes we say we are standing up "in our hearts." But God is telling us that He doesn't want only our hearts to "stand up." He wants us to physically say, "No!" to the spirit of the world and "Yes!" to His will.

When we stand up for God, the Fourth Man is going to show up! The Son of God will stand with us in the fire. If we compromise, we will die alone.

Let us be a part of this new breed of leadership that God is raising up. Let's recognize who we are in God. Let's be bold and preach an uncompromised message. Let's be willing to pay the price to reach our generation.

—Adapted from a message given at CFNI—Dallas.

Nevers Mumba is a Zambian politician and minister. He once pastored the Victory Bible Church and directed the Victory Institute of Biblical Studies in Kitwe, Zambia. Dr. Mumba served as Vice-President of Zambia and as Zambia's High Commissioner to Canada.

Reprinted by permission: Christ for the Nations

CFNI, P.O. Box 769000, Dallas, TX 75376-9000, 800-933-2364

ZOE COURSE DESCRIPTIONS

"My sheep hear My voice, and I know them, and they follow Me." John 10:27 (KJV)

HEARING COURSES

Hearing God's Voice

In this course, everyone is encouraged to participate by applying the principles they read in scripture in order to learn to recognize when the Holy Spirit is speaking. The inner knowing, inner voice, and the authoritative voice of the Holy Spirit are discussed, as well as other manifestations of the Holy Spirit. The Lord is personal and unique, and desires to communicate with each one of His sheep in a personal and unique manner! (This course is a prerequisite for all the following courses except for How to Hear God's Voice —In Marriage.)

How To Hear God's Voice—In Christ

In the Hearing God's Voice course we learned how to hear God as individuals, whereas in the In Christ course, we learn how the body of Christ operates together under His direction and to His glory. We look at Romans 12 and examine the motive gifts that determine our individual bents. This study enables us to understand, appreciate and love each other. We also look at the Trinity and how they operate together. We learn about the precious person of the Holy Spirit and how He teaches, guides and comforts us. We also learn about the gifts of the Holy Spirit in 1 Corinthians 12 and 14 brought about as the Holy Spirit moves through us. Participants have remarked that this course has enabled them to see people the way God sees them and how they fit in the body of Christ.

How To Hear God's Voice—In Marriage

This course is based on the love relationship God had with mankind in the very beginning. We examine our attitudes toward each other and how they reflect the greatest love of all, the love of Christ. Do we love and honor each other with the unconditional love that our Lord Jesus had for us while dying on the cross? As in previous courses, we examine scripture, seek the Lord, and ask Him, "How can I better serve and love my spouse?" We discover how we complete each other, not compete with each other.

How To Hear God's Voice—In the Family

In today's society we see the growing deterioration of the family. Parents are confused about what the Bible teaches on family issues. During this course we examine scriptures and what it means to: "Train up a child [early childhood] in the way he should go [and in keeping with his individual bent], and when he is old [teen years can be the best] he will not depart from it." (AMP with additions)

KNOWING COURSES

How To Know God's Voice—In Intimate Friendship

Intimate Friendship with God! Can we experience such a relationship with the Creator of the universe? Here we examine what the Bible teaches us about the fear of the Lord, and how we can, indeed, have a deeper, more intimate relationship with Him. This is a very personal, yet freeing course on growing intimacy with God.

How To Know God's Voice—In Worship

The focus of this course is on ministering to the Lord. During our time together the Lord draws us corporately into His presence as we worship Him. We study what worship is, why we worship, and how we worship.

How To Know God's Voice—In His Presence

The Lord is calling each one of His sheep to come into His presence and to know Him in a deeper way. This course is not for the new believer nor the faint in heart. Those who are serious about knowing the Father in a more intimate way will find this course challenging but rewarding. Examining Jesus' last days on earth will direct us into the presence of the Lord. This course is for those who have completed other ZOE courses.

How To Know God's Voice—In the Coming of the Lord

Many are proclaiming dates and times when the Lord Jesus will return for His bride. This course is designed to focus on our preparation for His coming, not when He is coming, and to better understand the Lord's statement of Revelation 22:20: "Yes, I am coming." It is the goal of this course to prepare ourselves as the bride of Christ, with hearts that will respond with "Amen. Come, Lord Jesus."

FOLLOWING COURSES

How To Follow God's Voice—In Power

Evangelism is often thought of as a bad word! In this course we come to realize that God has a special plan for evangelism for us if we are only sensitive and obedient to His voice. Preparing your testimony, leading someone in salvation, and discipling others are a few of the topics discussed in this course. This is a real life-changer as we minister in "power evangelism!"

How To Follow God's Voice—In Healing

During this course we examine the scriptures in which Jesus healed the sick. The Holy Spirit highlights these passages as we study, and our faith increases! We realize that Jesus is the Healer, and we are simply His vessels as we listen to and follow His voice.

How To Follow God's Voice—In Intercession

Jesus is in constant intercession (Hebrews 7:25). As we come before Him in worship, intercession is a natural outflow of our relationship with Him. By yielding to the Holy Spirit, our ministry to others through intercession will increase.

How To Follow God's Voice—In Spiritual Warfare

As we come to know and recognize who our Lord is, He reveals to us who He is not! The tactics of Satan and our spiritual weapons are defined in this course. The Lord leads us in spiritual warfare as He enlists and mobilizes His army!

ONE-ON-ONE DISCIPLESHIP

Discipleship by the Word of God and the Power of the Holy Spirit

This 12-week course was developed by a disciple-maker after many years of successful one-on-one discipleship. Through this method the Holy Spirit is allowed to minister to the disciple through the Word and the encouragement of the disciple-maker. No other techniques or methods are used.

The entire course has been designed to enable individuals to feel confident in making disciples as directed by our Lord: *"Therefore go and make disciples of all nations ...."* Matthew 28:19.

Not only do the participants learn what discipleship means according to the Word of God, but they are encouraged to participate in a one-on-one discipleship program as part of the course. This training allows individuals to take great strides in their personal relationship with God and in ministry. It changes lives in a very simple, yet powerful way.

EVANGELISTIC OUTREACH — MINISTRY IN HOMES

Captivated by Their Character

This series of courses called Captivated by Their Character is designed to reach the unbeliever, new believer, and those needing a refresher course on the Trinity.

They are offered in a non-threatening, home atmosphere where every effort is made to make the participant feel comfortable with the material. For example, everyone uses the same Bible, referring to page numbers rather than books, no reading is required outside of the course, and they are given the freedom to express their inadequacies as a believer or non-believer.

Additional information is available on the ZOE website at www.zoeministries.org/zoe-courses

YOUNG ADULT HEARING GOD'S VOICE
MAGAZINE LIST

For your convenience we have included the following list of magazines from which this course's articles have been drawn. If you wish to receive these magazines on a regular basis, the subscription information below will help.

Charisma and Christian Life

Subscription Service Department   (800) 829-3346
P.O. Box 420234   www.charismamag.com
Palm Coast, FL 32142-0234

Christ For the Nations

P.O. Box 769000   (800) 933-CFNI
Dallas, TX 75376-9000   www.cfni.org

Worldwide Challenge

100 Lake Hart Drive, #1600   (800) 688-4992
Orlando, FL 32832-0100   www.worldwidechallenge.org

www.ingramcontent.com/pod-product-compliance
Lightning Source LLC
Chambersburg PA
CBHW081544040426
42448CB00015B/3212